What does it mean to have

Autism

Louise Spilsbury

Heinemann
LIBRARY

www.heinemann.co.uk/library
Visit our website to find out more information about Heinemann Library books.

To order:
 Phone 44 (0) 1865 888066
Send a fax to 44 (0) 1865 314091
 Visit the Heinemann Bookshop at www.heinemann.co.uk/library to browse our
catalogue and order online.

First published in Great Britain by Heinemann Library,
Halley Court, Jordan Hill, Oxford OX2 8EJ,
a division of Reed Educational and Professional Publishing Ltd.
Heinemann is a registered trademark of Reed Educational and Professional Publishing Ltd.

OXFORD MELBOURNE AUCKLAND
JOHANNESBURG BLANTYRE GABORONE
IBADAN PORTSMOUTH (NH) USA CHICAGO

Designed by AMR
Illustrated by David Woodroffe
Originated by Dot Gradations
Printed by Wing King Tong, Hong Kong.

ISBN 0 431 13925 3 (hardback)   ISBN 0 431 13932 6 (paperback)
06 05 04 03 02   06 05 04 03 02
10 9 8 7 6 5 4 3 2   10 9 8 7 6 5 4 3 2 1

British Library Cataloguing in Publication Data
Spilsbury, Louise
  What does it mean to have autism?
  1.Autism – Juvenile Literature
  I.Title II.Autism
  616.8'982

Acknowledgements
The publishers would like to thank the following for permission to reproduce photographs: Steve Hickey
Photography, pp. 5–6, 11, 14–15, 17–19, 22–24, 27; Telegraph Colour Library/Spencer Rowell, p.4.

The following pictures were taken on commission for Heinemann: Mark Azavedo, pp.12, 13; Trevor
Clifford, pp.28, 29; Maggie Milner, pp.20, 21; John Walmsley, pp.10, 16, 25, 26.

The pictures on the following pages were posed by models who do not have autism: 4, 10, 16, 25, 26.

Special thanks to: Afua, Richard, Kate, Niamh, Sean, Eoin and Mícheál; The Robert Ogden School and
pupils; Radlett Lodge School and pupils.

The publishers would also like to thank: The National Autistic Society, and Julie Johnson, PHSE
Consultant Trainer and Writer, for their help in the preparation of this book.

Contents

Any words appearing in the text in bold, **like this**, are explained in the Glossary.

What is autism?

Autism is a **condition** that affects the way a person communicates and gets on with other people. If there is a child in your school who has autism they may sometimes find it hard to say what they mean, or they may find it difficult to understand what other people mean. Children with autism are just as clever as other people, it is just that they see the world slightly differently.

Every child with autism is different and autism affects their lives in different ways. Most find it hard to make sense of the world around them in three main ways.

- **Communication** – they may have some kind of difficulty speaking or listening to other people.
- Understanding – they may have some kind of difficulty understanding other people or their feelings.
- Imagination – they find it hard to think of different ways of doing things, or to imagine how other people feel.

Many children with autism find the world around them a confusing place at times.

4

In the same way that each of us is unique, each person who has autism is an individual. Their autism is a part of who they are, and their behaviour and particular difficulties are different from those of anyone else.

Doctors may use the term 'autistic spectrum disorder' rather than autism. 'Spectrum' simply means 'range', and they use this word to explain that there is a range of different types and levels of autism. Some children have a lot of difficulties. They may speak very little and stay in their own world most of the time. Most children with autism go to ordinary schools, and talk and learn like others their age. They may simply have trouble understanding people at times, or prefer to be alone rather than involved in other people's games. Otherwise they lead full and active lives, just like everyone else.

Asperger syndrome

Asperger syndrome is a kind of autism. Children with Asperger syndrome usually have fewer problems with speaking and learning than other children with autism. They may, however, have difficulties understanding what people mean or how they feel. For example, when most people talk to someone, they can tell how that person feels as much by the look on their face as by what they say. People with Asperger syndrome may find it hard to spot and understand signals like these.

Common difficulties

Even though most people with autism share common difficulties, the way in which each person is affected may be very different.

Communication

Many children with autism do not start using words as soon as other children. Some may not learn to talk until they are much older, and others never speak at all. Many children with autism **communicate** well, although they may concentrate on a few favourite subjects. They may get confused about what people mean when they speak, and sometimes may appear not to be listening.

Understanding

Some children with autism find it hard to know how to behave with other people. Many find it hard to understand what someone else is thinking or feeling. This means they sometimes behave in ways that seem

Many children with autism are good with figures. They may enjoy particular subjects at school, such as maths.

unsuitable, like being very upset if a teacher just raises their voice a little. Some children who have autism seem to react to things in an exaggerated way, perhaps laughing uncontrollably at something that most other people only find a little bit funny.

Imagination

Many children with autism understand and learn facts and figures easily. Some, however, have trouble using their imagination. They may have difficulty with understanding stories or poems. It also means they may have difficulty imagining how other people feel. They may have trouble thinking of a different way of doing something or solving a problem.

Some ways children with autism behave

These are some of the things children with autism do. Not all children with autism do all these things, and many stop doing these things as they get older. Children with autism may:
- copy words exactly
- talk about one topic all the time
- behave oddly at times
- handle or spin objects
- not play with other children
- like things to be the same
- seem not to care sometimes
- join in only if an adult insists and helps
- talk but does not listen
- not always look at people when talking
- laugh and giggle at unsuitable times
- BUT may do some things very well and quickly.

What causes autism?

Most children with autism find the world a confusing place at times. This is because the parts of their **brain** which take in information and make sense of it work slightly differently from other people's.

How your brain works

Your brain is the control centre of your body. It controls the rest of your body and makes sure that all the different parts work properly together. It controls how you think, learn and feel.

Your brain is connected to the other parts of your body by **nerves**. These are a bit like telephone lines. Messages from all parts of your body travel from the nerves to the **spinal cord** (which runs inside your backbone) and up to the brain.

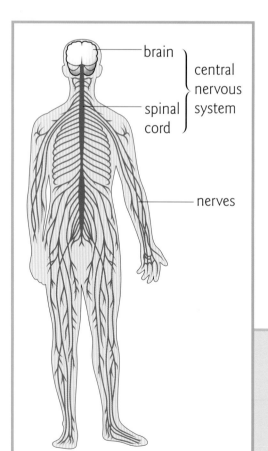

brain ⎫
⎬ central nervous system
spinal cord ⎭

nerves

Messages from your brain travel to the spinal cord and on to the rest of your body. For example, if you rest your hand on something dangerously hot, **nerve endings** in your hand carry a pain message to the spinal cord and on to the brain. The brain sends a message back to tell you to remove your hand. All this happens at lightning speed.

*Your brain, spinal cord and the network of nerves in your body make up your **central nervous system**.*

How autism affects the brain

Different parts of your brain deal with different kinds of messages. Some parts are involved in responding to signals from your **senses** to allow you to see, hear, touch, speak and move. Other parts are involved in thinking and memory. If a part of a person's brain develops in a slightly different way to usual, it may work slightly differently. For example, if the part that controls a person's muscles does not develop properly, they may not be able to move their limbs, but they are able to do everything else.

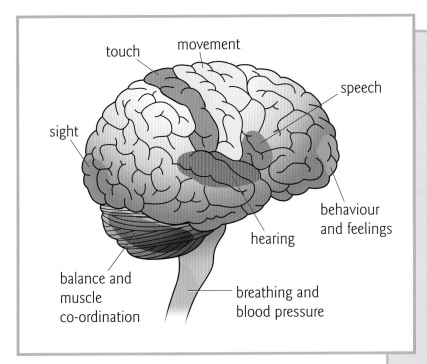

touch
movement
speech
sight
behaviour and feelings
hearing
balance and muscle co-ordination
breathing and blood pressure

Different parts of the brain are responsible for different jobs in the body. In a child with autism it may be that a part of their brain develops in a slightly different way. Or it may be that the signals that pass from one part to another do not connect in the usual way.

Scientists believe that in children with autism the parts of the brain that deal with the way they take in information, work out what it means, and then decide what they think and feel about it don't develop in the usual way. This explains why they may have trouble making sense of the world. People with autism are usually as clever as everyone else, because other parts of their brain are not affected.

Diagnosing autism

It is very difficult to be sure that a person has autism. It is a tricky **condition** to **diagnose** because there is no one thing that all children with autism have. It is not like having chicken-pox, where all children have itchy spots. Instead, doctors have to study what a child has been like from birth onwards. They talk about this with the child's parents and carers.

The doctors also meet with the child and watch how they react in lots of different situations. Early signs they look out for include the child not responding when their name is called, not looking at people when they talk to them, and copying other people. Doctors may also do tests to rule out other conditions that may make the child behave in similar ways.

*Doctors and **health visitors** may spot early signs of autism when parents bring their children in for routine health checks.*

Facts about autism

- Autism affects many more boys than girls.
- Around one in every 100 people is affected by some form of autism.
- Usually, autism is something babies are born with.
- A **diagnosis** of autism helps. It is easier for someone with autism if people understand their difficulties.

Getting help

It is important that when anything is wrong with any of us we get it checked out as soon as possible. However, sometimes people don't like the idea of being told there is something different about them. They may be afraid that other people will call them names because of their condition. This is understandable. However, it is important to find out what is wrong so something can be done to help.

Imagine that someone cannot see very well, and they do not want to go to the optician because they don't want to wear glasses. Without glasses they will miss out on so much and life will be much more difficult for them. This is the same with autism. Once autism is diagnosed, children and their families can be given the support they need to make the most of their lives.

It is important that autism is recognized as early in a person's life as possible. Then, with proper support, they can learn how to deal with any difficulties they have and to make the most of the things they are good at.

Meet Abena and Afua

My name is Abena and my daughter Afua is six years old. My husband and I were told Afua had autism when she was three years old. Up until that time we had no real idea what autism was. We were just concerned that Afua did not speak. At first she had hearing tests, but her hearing appeared to be fine. So she had some sessions with a **speech therapist**, who tried to help her to talk. But still she did not speak. She could sing the words of songs she heard, but she never said 'mummy' or 'daddy' or any other words to us.

Finally we saw a **psychiatrist**, who asked us lots of questions about how Afua played and if she had particular ways of doing things. We told him that she liked to play alone and that she had set ways of doing several things. For instance, she would always line her dolls up in a certain way or get upset if we didn't walk down the supermarket aisle in one direction. We thought his questions seemed odd. It wasn't until we were told she had autism and we began to read about it that we realized that these things were classic signs of autism.

The first thing we sorted out was Afua's speech. It turned out that she had very sensitive hearing. She had some special treatment to retrain her ears to block out unnecessary background noise so she could concentrate on speech. With help from the speech therapist, she learnt to say about 50 words within two months. She used to have tantrums because she got so frustrated and angry when we didn't understand what she wanted. Now she can tell us herself.

We also work on teaching her how to be safe, and how to behave with other people. For example, it took a long time to teach her not to run off in the street, because she didn't understand roads were dangerous. I also help her to control behaviour that is unacceptable, like hitting other kids. But I don't want to change her. Autism is not a problem. It's just that Afua sees the world differently to most people.

When you talk to adults with autism they say they have no wish to see the world the way other people do. They just want to be understood and respected for the way they are. Afua is fantastic! She is fun and fascinating and I wouldn't want her any other way.

Helping with autism

Autism is not like an illness, which you can put right by taking a course of medicine. It is a part of who the person is. It affects how they think and feel. Most young people deal with the difficulties caused by autism with other people's support and understanding, and through their own hard work and determination.

Young people work with special teachers and with their families. They learn to control the ways of behaving that cause difficulties and they learn to find ways of **communicating** successfully. Sometimes, even when children learn the right way to behave they cannot keep it up all the time. If they slip up, it is not because they are not trying hard enough – after all, no one expects a ballet dancer to dance perfectly every minute of the day. It can take a lot of effort to behave as other people expect.

Doing exercise helps all of us stay healthy and feel good about ourselves. For young people with autism, exercise also helps them to get rid of some of the anxiety and frustration they sometimes feel.

Special interests

Some people with autism cope by turning their difficulties into advantages. For example, many young people develop a special interest or hobby. For people with autism this often involves facts and figures. It may be something to do with trains and train timetables, or collecting and arranging facts about their favourite pop group. These special interests can cause difficulties for some people with autism because they find it hard to talk or think about anything else.

Having a special interest or hobby can be a great thing, whether or not you have autism.

This need not be a problem, however, as they can use their special interests to help them with their schoolwork. For instance, if they have trouble getting into books, they could find a book that is about their favourite subject to help them with their reading skills. As they grow up, many people with autism seek jobs that are connected with that interest or which use the skills they gained while working on their hobby.

Communication

Everyone needs to be able to communicate in some way. We communicate with other people to share thoughts, ideas, needs and feelings. Many children with autism who use little or no speech can learn with the help of a **speech therapist**. This is someone who can teach them how to talk and how to join in conversations by listening and replying to people at the right time and in the right way.

The problem most children with autism have with communication is that they find it hard to express themselves. They may speak in one tone, so that their voices do not go up and down as most people's do when they talk. They may also have difficulty understanding when to ask questions or what people mean when they make certain faces. Just like everyone else, children with autism go on learning as they grow up. With help, they gradually learn to speak and communicate more clearly.

Young people with autism who can talk may need some help with other skills to do with communicating. They may need to learn how to look at people when they are being spoken to, and how to ask and answer questions at the right times.

Sometimes people with autism have difficulty working out what people mean, especially when they tell a joke. But they'll get the punch line if it's explained in a different way!

Coping with confusion

Many people with autism speak perfectly well, but may have trouble understanding some expressions people use. Because they find it hard to imagine other possible meanings, they take some things literally. So, if another child says, 'That new teacher nearly bit my head off', the child with autism may be really worried. They don't understand 'bit my head off' to mean 'shout crossly', as most people do. They think the words mean exactly what they say – that the teacher might really bite someone's head off! This may seem strange, but imagine how it must feel. Think about all the phrases that we use every day that could cause confusion, like 'die laughing' and 'make friends'.

As people with autism get older they learn what more and more of these odd phrases mean. They may still be caught out when someone uses an expression they have not heard before, but they usually learn ways of dealing with this. They may simply ask the speaker to explain what they mean.

Managing autism

Most of us like to know what our day will be like when we wake up each morning. This is the same for children with autism. They like order in their life so they feel secure. They like to keep things in the same place and they like to follow set routines. Sudden changes to a routine, such as a change of teacher if one is off sick, may easily upset them. It is hard for any of us to settle down, for example to schoolwork, if we are anxious.

This aspect of autism is easy to manage. Parents or teachers can help the child make a timetable showing what will happen each day and what they will need for each activity, like a PE kit for a games lesson at school. Then if there are any changes to the timetable, they can be explained well in advance and written on the timetable so children have time to get used to the change. If a change happens suddenly, most children can accept it if people take time to explain the reasons for it.

Having a timetable to remind us what we are supposed to be doing every day is a good idea for everyone, not just young people with autism.

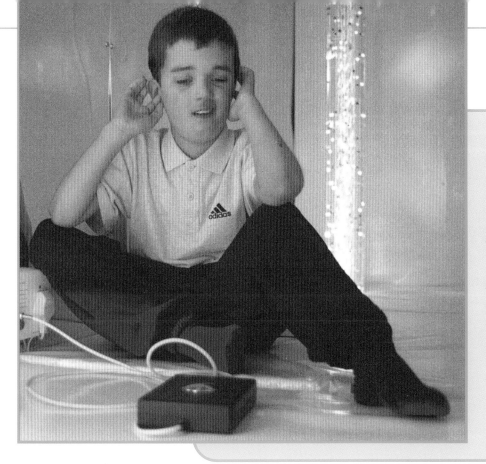

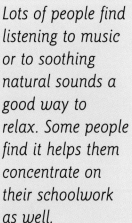

Lots of people find listening to music or to soothing natural sounds a good way to relax. Some people find it helps them concentrate on their schoolwork as well.

Other ways of helping

If you get cross or frustrated when something goes wrong, is there something special you do to help you relax? Many children with autism have times when they get very cross or angry. When this happens, they may use different tactics to help them calm down. Some like to go off somewhere quiet on their own. Others may listen to music or special soothing sounds that they know will help them wind down.

A lot of the time, coping with autism is really about finding different ways of doing things. For instance, some young people with autism have difficulty writing neatly and presenting their work well. This can be very frustrating, especially if you know it is really a good piece of work. Lots of people with autism do their homework on a computer. Typing is often much easier than writing and the end result is much more satisfying.

Meet Richard and Sue

My name is Sue and I'm Richard's mum. Richard is twelve. He was **diagnosed** as having **Asperger syndrome** when he was ten. We were relieved to finally have an explanation for the difficulties Richard had been dealing with his whole life.

Richard had been finding school hard. He could do the work, but he didn't always follow what the teacher was saying and he got upset if he was teased. One reason for this is because he often misunderstands what people mean. For example, when I tried to get him to stand up for himself against the bullies, he said 'Why do I have to *stand* up?' He takes things to mean exactly what they say.

Now we teach Richard at home. We help him by finding ways of explaining things so he'll understand them. We also try to teach him how to get on with other people – simple things like remembering to say 'thank you' when he should. He likes to know what is going to happen ahead of time and he likes to do some things in a certain way. We stick to a regular weekly routine to help him feel settled.

Life is much easier now we know Richard has autism. We can get on with helping him make the most of his abilities.

My name is Richard. I know all about autism. It's OK, but sometimes it can be really horrible and really hard. I can cope with it sometimes, but sometimes it gets the better of me. I get frustrated and then I go mad when I let it out. Sometimes I get really angry and I shout and chuck things around. Then I feel better afterwards.

Learning at home is better for me because if I need help I can just ask my mum and she comes. I didn't feel comfortable asking the teacher at school. English is my favourite subject. I like science because I'm learning about the planets. I don't like spelling – not because it's hard, but because it's boring.

I've got a new room. If I get angry I can go in there and watch TV and play on my PlayStation. I like roller-skating, squash and football. I support Liverpool. I also learnt to unicycle and juggle. I can even do them both at the same time! I did a sponsored unicycle ride to raise money for our local autism group. I raised nearly £500 and I'm really proud of that.

Living with autism

One of the challenges of living with autism is that other people cannot see that a child is dealing with difficulties. Children with autism look just like other children. They do not have a bandaged leg or a wheelchair to tell people something is wrong. So when a child with autism gets upset or angry in a situation most children could deal with, other people may not understand. They may think the child is just being naughty or difficult.

The reality is that the child has a **condition** that makes it very hard for them to learn the accepted way of behaving towards other people. It is perfectly reasonable that children with autism feel frustrated sometimes when things seem to be going wrong, or upset when their routine is disrupted.

Being able to talk to other people who have similar difficulties as you can be a great help. Some young people who have autism meet at clubs or groups near their homes, or via the Internet.

Many young people who have autism find their own way of doing things and a way of life they feel comfortable with. They say they would not want to lose their special way of looking at the world even if they could.

How does it feel?

Most children with autism have times when it gets them down and they feel sad or angry. They may find it hard to make friends who are willing to take time to understand them. They may get frustrated if they get behind with schoolwork because they cannot quite follow what the teacher is saying.

However, as many people with autism get older, they decide that they would not change the way they are. They find ways of fitting in with what other people expect some of the time, but otherwise they are happy as they are. They feel that it is up to other people to accept them as the individuals they are. For example, many people with autism like to go off on their own a lot. They may be annoyed when other people suggest that they are missing out or think they are lonely. All they are really doing is what makes them feel happy.

At school

Many children with autism go to ordinary schools. They may be perfectly happy without any extra help, or they may need some support. It may be that they need an adult to work with them while they are in class to check that they understand the work they are set. Or they may need some help mixing with other children at break-times and lunchtimes.

Most of us would give up listening and go off into our own worlds if someone was talking about a complicated subject we did not understand. Some children with autism just need someone to explain things in a way they can understand.

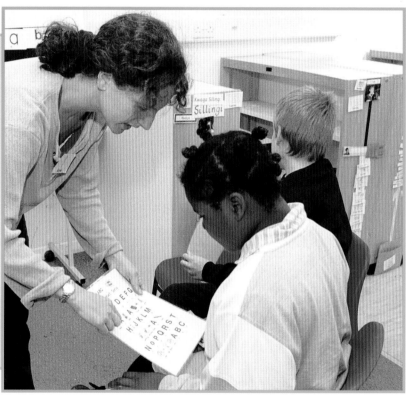

Some children with autism need more support and they may go to a class or school especially for children who have autism. They may be happier at a school just for children with autism, because things are possible there that might be difficult at an ordinary school. For example, some children with autism become anxious at break-times when everyone is running around. At a special school they may be able to take short breaks at the end of lessons instead, in a quiet room where there are not too many other people around.

Other people

Some children at school tease or pick on children with autism. This may be because they sometimes behave differently and this makes them stand out. No one should ever have to put up with bullying. They or their friends should tell a teacher or other adult who they trust so they can sort it out.

People who pick on someone who has autism don't understand what autism is. They mistakenly believe that children with autism are just using it as an excuse to be naughty or difficult. Or perhaps they think that children with autism don't understand they are being teased, so it does not matter if they pick on them. Of course this is not true. Some children with autism feel better if their teacher or parent gives a talk to their class, to explain what autism is and to put right any wrong ideas that people may have about it.

In some schools children with autism have a 'buddy' – an older child who offers to hang around with them in the playground, to help them understand the rules of any games they don't understand, or to make sure they are not bullied.

At home

We all like to go home at the end of the day to relax and unwind. This is especially important for young people with autism because they may have to make a special effort throughout the school day to behave in the way people expect them to. During the day they may also have to face unexpected changes to their routine or the way things are set out in class, which can be upsetting.

At home they can have things as they like them. We all have little routines we like to follow when we get home. Perhaps you always have a drink and a snack in front of the television. For young people with autism it is just the same. They may always like to eat their dinner in exactly the same spot, or sit in a particular chair. It is just that they may get a bit more upset than others if their routine is disrupted.

Many children with autism say they think in pictures, not words. Some say their thoughts are like videotapes playing in their mind. Many find watching cartoons on TV relaxing because stories made up of images are easy to follow.

26

Brothers and sisters

Home life can be tricky for brothers and sisters of people who have autism. They may have to deal with behaviour that can be annoying. For instance, they may have to stop playing board games because the child with autism is losing and cannot control their feelings of frustration. It can seem unfair that when they do something wrong they get told off, whereas the child with autism does not. They learn to understand that the difference is that they know when they are doing something naughty, while the child with autism does not realise.

Yet, most people say that they would not change their **sibling**. Many say having a brother or sister with autism makes them more mature. They often have a better understanding of other people and can be much more tolerant of people's differences than other people their age. When they stand up for a sibling who is being teased it can be difficult, but most say that it feels good to know they have made a stand and done what is right.

Lots of people say there are many good points about having a brother or sister who has autism. One is that it makes them look at the world in a whole new way.

Meet the Mason family

There are five young people in the Mason family. Kate is fifteen, Niamh is thirteen, the twins Sean and Eoin are twelve, and Mícheál is ten. The three boys in the family have autism.

Kate: Family life was affected a bit more when the boys were younger. They would try to run away when we went out or they would hit out at people. Things are better now because they understand more. Sean likes going shopping on Saturdays and then to look at fish in a tropical fish shop. Eoin has just started at my school. He is clever but he gets some help from a teacher who stays with him in school. I don't really think about autism – they're just our brothers.

Niamh: Sometimes people say about Sean, 'What's wrong with your brother?' I just say, 'Nothing. He just finds it hard to talk.' Lately, though, Sean has started to talk. I've helped him get the words out. He just pointed at things he wanted before. Now he can say mostly what he wants.

If Sean gets fed up, I cheer him up by listening to tapes of nice music with him, or to the sea or birds singing. It's a good way of calming down. He gives me a hug if I'm in a bad mood. I wouldn't want to change my brothers even if I could.

Eoin: Autism changes the way you think about the world. Sometimes people don't make friends with me. That annoys me because I'm not disabled, I'm just like normal people. But I've got a group of friends at school and I've made lots of friends through the Internet.

I collect Pokémon cards and I like watching cartoons. My favourite lesson at school is art. I'm good at drawing. I like IT as well. I like designing things. I designed a big banner for the school.

Mícheál: I like playing on the computer. My favourite game is Grand Prix racing. I'm in my last year of primary school. At school I like going outside, and doing maths. I'm good at maths.

I like swimming at our swimming pool. It has this big slide and when you get to the bottom you go falling into the pool. Eating is my favourite thing. When we have sweetcorn I usually eat four or even six!

Sean: I like sweets, music, swimming and cooking. I love my brothers and sisters and I like cuddling and kissing them.

29

Glossary

Asperger syndrome name for a particular kind of autism. People with Asperger syndrome have fewer difficulties with communication, understanding and imagination than others who have an autistic spectrum disorder.

autistic spectrum disorder term used to explain the fact that there is a range of different kinds and levels of autism ('spectrum' simply means 'range')

brain control centre of the body. It controls the rest of the body and how we think, learn and feel.

central nervous system the way the brain and nerves are linked together by the spinal cord within the backbone

communication ways of telling other people what we think and how we feel, and to understand how they think and feel

condition when someone has a lifelong difficulty, such as autism

diagnose when a doctor decides what disease or condition a person has

diagnosis when a doctor tells someone what disease or condition they have

health visitor specially trained nurse who checks that children up to the age of five are healthy and growing properly and visits sick or old people to check if they need help

nerves parts of the body that take messages to and from the brain with information from our five senses (sight, hearing, touch, taste and smell)

nerve endings group of nerves at certain points of our body, such as the ends of our fingers

psychiatrist doctor who is expert at knowing how a person's behaviour and feelings might be affected by a condition like autism

scientists people who do experiments and study people and the world around us to find out how we feel, and to understand how they think and feel

senses our senses give us information we need to know about the world around us – eyes see, ears hear, tongues taste, noses smell and skin touches

sibling brother or sister

speech therapist person who is specially trained to help others learn to speak when they are having difficulties

spinal cord part of the body that links the brain to the nerves all around the body. It is protected by the backbone.

Useful books and addresses

BOOKS

Hangman, Julia Jarman, Andersen Press, 2000

Truth or Dare, Celia Rees, Macmillan, 2000

Body Systems: Thinking and feeling, Angela Royston, Heinemann Library, 1996

Look at Your Body: Brain and Nerves, Steve Parker, Watts, 1998

Understanding Your Brain, Rebecca Treays, Usborne Publishing, 1995

Think About Having a Learning Disability, Margaret and Peter Flynn, Belitha Press, 1998

My Brother is Different, Louise Gorrod, National Autistic Society, 1997

What is Asperger Syndrome and How Will it Affect Me? NAS Autism Helpline, National Autistic Society, 1998

ORGANIZATIONS AND WEBSITES

The National Autistic Society
Headquarters
393 City Road
London EC1V 1NG
Telephone: 020 7833 2299
Website: www.nas.org.uk
E-mail: nas@nas.org.uk
Autism Helpline telephone: 0870 600 8585
This society supports people with autism and their families across the UK. They also support local groups.

IN AUSTRALIA

National Association for Autism
c/o Autism Association of NSW
PO Box 361
Forestville NSW 2087
Telephone (02) 9452 3447
Fax: (02) 9451 3447
E-mail: aanswnet@ozemail.com.au
Website: www.autismaus.com.au

Index

Titles in the *What does it mean to have/be* series include:

Hardback   0 431 13924 5

Hardback   0 431 13921 0

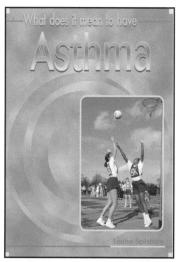

Hardback   0 431 13920 2

Hardback   0 431 13922 9

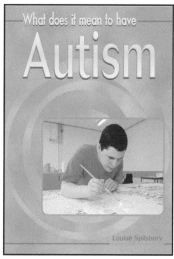

Hardback   0 431 13925 3

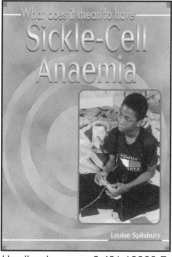

Hardback   0 431 13923 7

Find out about the other titles in this series on our website www.heinemann.co.uk/library